Library of Congress Cataloging-in-Publication Data available

ISBN 978-0-545-88857-8

10 9 8 7 6 5 4 3 2 1   15 16 17 18 19

Printed in the U.S.A.   40

First edition, 2015

Written by Joe Funk
with Trevor Talley

Creative Director: Jason Hinman
Special thanks to: Hana Bae, Charlie Scibetta, Stephenie Ly, Marc Boese,
Dan Pantumsinchai, Noriko Matsunaga, Brent Coyle, Tiffany O'Brien, Scott Jobe,
Beth Dunfey, Amy Levenson, Heather Dalgleish, and Grace Liu.

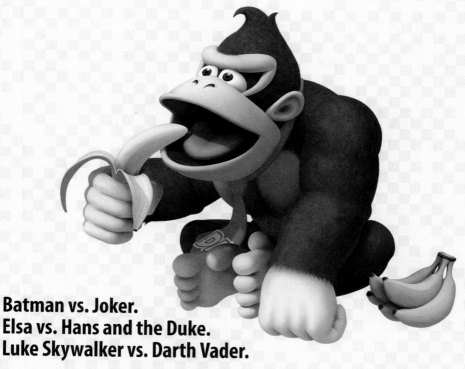

Batman vs. Joker.
Elsa vs. Hans and the Duke.
Luke Skywalker vs. Darth Vader.

Everyone loves a good showdown. And every medium has epic examples.

Video games have their own homegrown heroes: There have been countless face-offs between the fittest and fastest, the smartest and strongest, the most lethal and the most lucky.

In fact, showdowns between heroes and bosses have been a cornerstone of video games since the very beginning, with some reaching legendary status.

This book highlights some of the most famous rivals and archrivals in video-game history, with profiles of the combatants and descriptions of their duels.

Since interacting with the characters is a big part of the appeal of video games, we're not here to spoil any outcomes—after all, it's up to YOU to decide the victor when playing these games.

Our aim is to tell each story and explain why each showdown has etched itself into the indelible digital lore of video games. So read on and see who made it onto our list. Whether it's a game you've played or have never tried, this book is your ultimate fight card for video gaming's merriest mayhem.

WHAT'S INSIDE

Images courtesy of Nintendo.

Images courtesy of Nintendo.

If there were a title for the most epic showdowns in

video-game history, it would go to the famous and fierce struggles between Mario and his pals and the forces of Bowser, Wario, and the other villains of the Mushroom Kingdom universe. In fact, there are more than 150 games featuring Mario, and titanic showdowns between the heroes and villains of the Mushroom Kingdom universe have raged across nearly all of them. Can you imagine how many hours of fighting that adds up to? Talk about epic!

The many clashes between Mario and his nemeses are a large part of what has made this the most popular and successful series in video-game history. The battle goes back all the way to the very first title that included Mario, the *Donkey Kong* arcade cabinet, which was released in 1982. In that game, we see Mario using his signature jumping abilities to navigate a treacherous series of ladders and steel girders in order to rescue a pretty lady stolen away by the villainous Donkey Kong.

MARIO, FRIENDS & FOES

The game was a smashing success, and it led to a massive expansion of the Mushroom Kingdom universe with the next two titles, *Mario Bros.* and *Super Mario Bros.* It was in these historic games that Mario became the character we know and love today, and where many of his friends and foes were introduced. Now the characters of Mario, Princess Peach, Toad, Bowser, Wario, Donkey Kong, and others are known all over the world. They are some of the most recognizable and beloved characters ever created.

Not only are the characters adorable, they're also dangerous fighters! So for this showdown, we're going to look at Mario and two of his helpful pals against three of their biggest, baddest rivals. It's one heck of a contest!

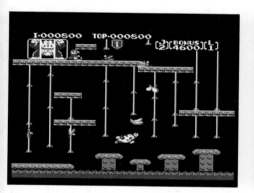
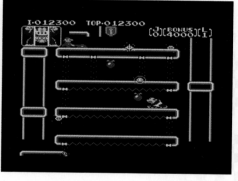
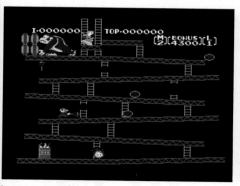
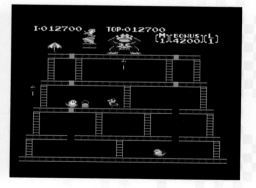

Images courtesy of Nintendo.

MARIO

The Hero and one of the World's Favorite Video-Game Characters

Strengths

- Fearless in the face of adversity
- Mighty jumping ability
- Jumping attacks, including the jump-stomp, the spin-jump, and the ground-pound
- An array of awesome power-ups that give Mario special abilities, such as the famous Super Mushroom, which lets Mario grow to twice his size; the Fire Flower, which allows him to shoot scorching fireballs; and the Tanooki Suit, which provides Mario with an animal disguise and the power of flight, among other things
- Tons of talented friends

Mario is one of the most recognizable characters in the world, with his signature red hat emblazoned with a big "M," red shirt, blue overalls, and white gloves.

Mario's quests are usually in the name of rescuing Princess Peach or defeating some threat to his colorful universe. Sometimes, though, he just wants to play a round of golf or race cars. The list of fun and challenging activities Mario has tried ranges from painting to playing board games to just about everything else!

MARIO, FRIENDS & FOES

Across all his adventures, Mario has proven that he fears no danger: He has taken on many foes to protect his friends and his land. Mario's main ability is his powerful jump, which he uses to smash his attackers into the ground. This skill is so important that his character was originally named Jumpman. Sometimes in the games, Mario has to prove who he is by jumping for people, which he always does with gusto.

Mario's biggest strength, however, is the power of his many friendships. Through his countless adventures, Mario has made hundreds of friends with different powers, and it is often with their help that he overcomes adversity and wins the day.

Images courtesy of Nintendo.

MARIO'S PALS

Mario has many cool friends, some of whom have become almost as famous as Mario himself! While it would take a whole book to talk about all of Mario's pals, there are a few core friends who join Mario on his quests and prove to be formidable fighters themselves:

Luigi

Luigi was first introduced in the game titled *Mario Bros*. Since then, he has been at Mario's side, battling villains in the Mushroom Kingdom universe with as much skill and fearlessness as his more famous brother. Luigi is shy, quiet, and often overshadowed by his sibling, but he's actually quite talented. His jumping ability surpasses Mario's, and his all-around skills let him overcome any problem. He's a bit cowardly and really afraid of ghosts. Even so, in the Luigi's Mansion games, he was charged with cleaning up poltergeist problems.

Princess Peach

Princess Peach started out as a "damsel in distress," the character who needed to be rescued by Mario and his brother. However, Princess Peach is rarely helpless: She is smart and resourceful, and has become a skilled heroine herself in more recent games. Outfitted in her pink-and-white dress, she has a pink parasol that she uses to float over foes.

Images courtesy of Nintendo.

Yoshi

Mario's best friend and traveling companion, Yoshi has a long, sticky tongue and eternally happy attitude. One or another of the many Yoshis has been with Mario since his early adventures, including when they rescued Baby Mario and Baby Luigi from Koopas. Since then, Mario and the Yoshis have been inseparable, whether playing tennis or riding over the heads of Koopas. Yoshi uses his tongue to eat things, transform them, or spit them at foes. Yoshi is also an expert jumper capable of doing the Flutter Jump, which allows him to remain in the air over long distances.

Toad

Toads are servants at Princess Peach's castle in the Mushroom Kingdom. Toads give off a strong sense of peace but are no strangers to adventure. Most feature white heads with red polka dots, but there are other types as well, including Captain Toad, self-proclaimed leader of the Toad Brigade. Toads are some of Mario's greatest allies. They are firm defenders of the Mushroom Kingdom, where Princess Peach rules and many of Mario's adventures take place. They are strong and fast—and they can jump. They are also excellent kart drivers.

Mario's Foes

Mario has battled many colorful adversaries over the years, including hundreds of villains from dozens of species. Some have dared to face the mighty Mario more than once, and a few have become archrivals of our hero.

Images courtesy of Nintendo.

MARIO, FRIENDS & FOES

Strengths:

- Fire breath
- Very strong
- Has a spiky, tough protective shell that is hard to damage
- Uses many weapons, including hammers
- Can appear in different sizes—sometimes gigantic!
- Has an army of Koopas and other creatures at his command

BOWSER
King of the Koopas

Bowser is the King of the Koopas and Mario's eternal rival. He breathes fire, hurls hammers, and uses all sorts of weapons in the hope of taking out Mario. As his size suggests, he's immensely powerful. His plans aren't always the best, and sometimes he even finds himself on Mario's side.

Other villains:

Donkey Kong

Mario's original adversary, Donkey Kong has tremendous strength. He is fond of throwing barrels at those who stand against him.

Wario

A living embodiment of gross, this villain is jealous of Mario and loves money. He claims to have known Mario since childhood, but who can tell if that's true? Aside from adventuring, he's also the chairman of game maker WarioWare, Inc. He can also store up his trademark Wario Waft for explosive results in the Super Smash Bros. games. Did we mention he's gross?

MARIO, FRIENDS & FOES

SHOWDOWN

These characters have all faced one another in various combinations over 150 games, and many of their battles are among the most important in video-game history. Since we can only pick one epic showdown, we'll pick the game in which four of the heroes take on the game's most dastardly villain, Bowser: *Super Mario 3D World*.

In this game, Bowser is up to his old tricks again, stealing away the Sprixies. It is up to Mario, Luigi, Princess Peach, and Toad to go on a journey to rescue them.

The heroes fight their way to Bowser's castle, where they find the hulking King of the Koopas. The friends do battle on a road above a river of molten lava, the ideal location for the heat-loving Bowser.

Images courtesy of Nintendo.

Mario and friends knock out the fearsome Bowser, who plummets into the lava below. Before they can celebrate their victory, though, Bowser flies up out of the lava and snatches back the Sprixies. He carries them to his giant castle, where they are locked high up in a castle tower. Mario, Luigi, Princess Peach, and Toad resolve to save the Sprixies from Bowser's evil clutches. They scramble up the side of the castle only to meet Bowser in a new, more ferocious form.

Can Mario and his companions stand up to the newest, fiercest Bowser? Will they save the Sprixies from the castle? Answer these questions yourself as you harness all the powers of Mario and his friends to save the Sprixies in *Super Mario 3D World* for the Wii U console!

Images courtesy of Nintendo.

Did you know that there once was a game that was so popular in arcades that there were multiple laws made to keep people from spending so much time playing it? A game that has been near the top of the list of the games that have made the most money in history for over 30 years? A game that was so popular that grocery stores started clearing out all of their food so that they could fill their buildings with these arcade machines?

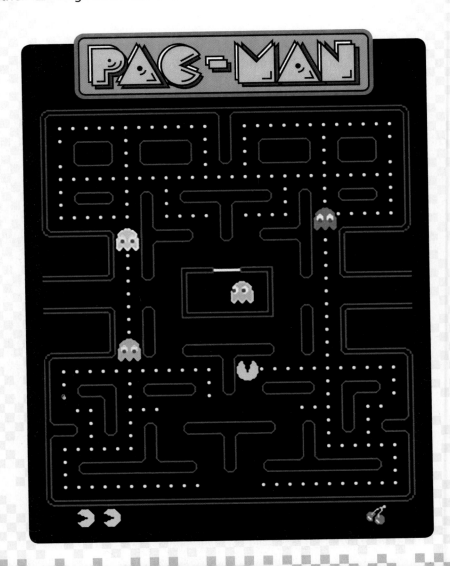

Another one of the most popular video games of all time is *Pac-Man*, which took the world by storm when it first came out in 1980. Pac-Man is a simple little yellow circle who moves through an arcade-size maze trying to evade or consume the four ghosts that pursue him. There's not much story to *Pac-Man*—it's all about the skills.

While *Pac-Man* doesn't have much of a plot, there are a lot of stories surrounding Pac-Man's design: Legend has it that Pac-Man's creator, Toru Iwatani, took his team out for pizza one night, and when one person took a slice, the shape for Pac-Man was born! Another story suggests that the shape is a rounded version of the Japanese symbol for *kuchi*, which means "mouth." The name Pac-Man comes from a Japanese slang word, *paku paku*, which is used to describe the motion of the mouth opening and closing while eating (like "chomp chomp"). Try it out; it's pretty fun to say.

As much as games like Grand Theft Auto or Call of Duty seem hugely popular, nothing compares with *Pac-Man* (except, perhaps, its predecessor *Space Invaders*).

Of course, what we're focused on in this book is the showdown in each game, and in Pac-Man's case, this little yellow guy's fight versus a flock of ghosts is exactly what made this game one of the most important, lovable games of all time.

Strengths

- The hungriest creature of all time; can eat forever!
- Can go in any direction in the maze
- Can shift directions on a dime
- Can consume power-ups to make the ghosts edible

PAC-MAN (aka Puck Man; Pakkuman)

When it comes to his endless quest to beat the ghosts, Pac-Man does have some interesting advantages. The biggest of these is that he is much quicker than his ghostly adversaries, so if you're careful, you can always avoid them. We say "always," and we mean that—if you're playing on an arcade machine. That's because it is possible for a player to "beat" the game by reaching the highest score on several consecutive levels so the game actually breaks! The first guy to do this was Billy Mitchell of Hollywood, Florida, who did it in about six hours in 1999, 19 years after the game was first released.

Pac-Man's other most noticeable advantage is his ability to eat power pellets, the much larger versions of the pac-dots on the screen. These guys famously cause all ghosts to turn a deep blue, move more slowly, and head in the opposite direction, away from Pac-Man. If the powered-up Pac-Man can catch up to a ghost, he can swallow it down and send it back to the center box, which we like to call "ghost jail." Another bit of trivia: This is the first time a "power-up" feature was included in a video game. It was inspired by the character Popeye the Sailor Man, who eats spinach and instantly gains incredible powers.

The final and perhaps most important advantage for Pac-Man is something most players don't know, even after 35 years of gaming. However, it is also one of the ghosts' greatest strengths. You'll have to check out the ghosts' profiles to find out Pac-Man's strange secret!

Strengths

- Can destroy Pac-Man on contact

- Outnumber Pac-Man four to one

- Can return after they've been eaten

- And one more . . .

RED GHOST
Name: Oikake (Chaser)
Nickname: Akabei (Red Guy)
English Name/Nickname: Shadow/Blinky
Behavior: Chases directly after Pac-Man, going straight for him

PINK GHOST
Name: Machibuse (Ambusher)
Nickname: Pinky
English Name/Nickname: Speedy/Pinky
Behavior: Tries to get to the space directly in front of Pac-Man's mouth, in whatever direction Pac-Man is facing

CYAN GHOST
Name: Kimagure (Fickle)
Nickname: Aosuke (Blue Guy)
English Name/Nickname: Bashful/Inky
Behavior: Like Pinky, Blue Guy tries to get to the space directly in front of Pac-Man's mouth

ORANGE GHOST
Name: Otoboke (Stupid)
Nickname: Guzuta (Slow Guy)
English Name/Nickname: Pokey/Clyde
Behavior: Chases Pac-Man but also tends to move toward the lower left-hand corner of the screen

THE GHOSTS

Shadow, Speedy, Bashful, and Pokey (aka Blinky, Pinky, Inky, and Clyde)

The biggest secret of *Pac-Man* is that each of the ghosts in the game moves in a very specific pattern, so the player can predict where the ghosts might move and use that against them. According to the game's designer, the ghosts' movements were hinted at in their original Japanese names, but when the names were changed for English speakers, the hints were lost. This piece of information has remained somewhat of a secret for decades. No longer, though, because here is a chart with their real names and what they do!

When the ghosts team up, their programmed behaviors make them move in patterns. They try to surround Pac-Man from different sides in an effort to trap him. The ghosts are pretty good at what they do—especially for a game designed when artificial intelligence and game characters were very simple.

However, it also makes the ghosts quite vulnerable to any Pac-Man player who is in the know—which is now YOU!

SHOWDOWN

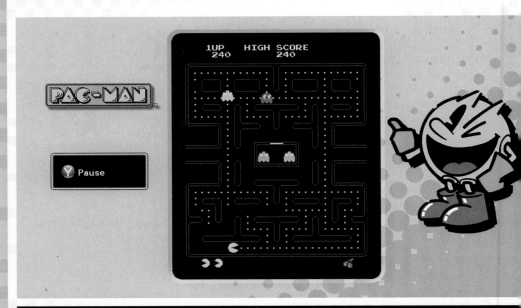

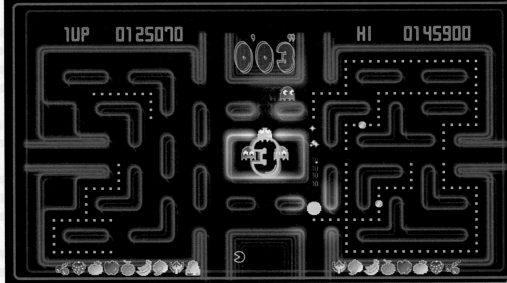

PAC-MAN vs. GHOSTS

Drop a quarter in the machine or push the START button, and that classic *Pac-Man* tune begins. It's time for one of the classic showdowns in all of video gaming: *Pac-Man vs. the Ghosts*.

Instantly the "waka-waka" (or "paku paku") starts as Pac-Man begins maneuvering his way through the maze, consuming all the pac-dots he can.

Blinky, the red ghost, is already out of ghost jail in the center of the maze, raring to go. It instantly takes off after Pac-Man, with pal Pinky close behind. Soon enough, Inky and Clyde make their exits as well, and the chase is on!

As Pac-Man darts about the course, chomping up pellets and frantically trying to keep space between himself and danger, the crafty ghosts start closing in on all sides. They're trying to pen Pac-Man into a tunnel or corner from which he cannot escape!

Will Pac-Man eat his fill, gobbling up every pellet and maybe a ghost or four? Or will the ghosts catch up to the little yellow guy and send him shrinking in despair? Only you can find out, so find yourself some Pac-Man action and be a part of one of the biggest, most important video games in history!

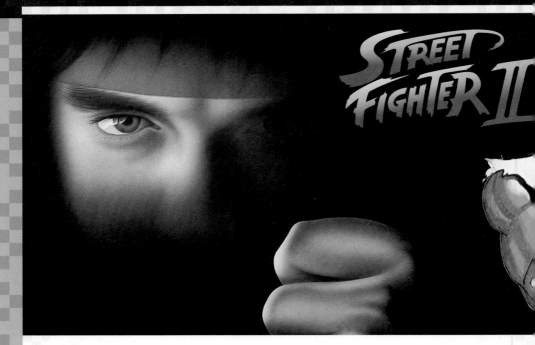

Without question, one of the most important video fighting games ever released was *Street Fighter*. Originally introduced as an arcade game in 1987, Street Fighter has cemented its status as the top fighting-game series, with title after blistering title of intense conflict. It is still considered the premier fighting game for professional tournaments today.

Originally, the two main fighters, Ryu and Ken, were the only playable characters in the game. The setting was an international martial arts tournament, in which Ryu and Ken competed against the best fighters in the world. While the original *Street Fighter* was a great game, *Street Fighter II* introduced new characters, more advanced moves, and different capabilities making Ryu and Ken's showdown something truly epic.

The ultimate game of one-on-one combat, *Street Fighter II* is legendary. Ryu and Ken are brothers in combat, yet fierce rivals. They trained together with the same martial arts master for many years, honing their skills and forming a deep bond. They share the same goal: to test their powers against as many fighters as possible and prove they are the best. This showdown pits these two warriors against each other—but only one can emerge the victor.

©CAPCOM

RYU
The Wandering Warrior
Driven on the Path of
Honor and Dedication

Strengths

- Master of Ansatsuken martial arts
- Dedicated to being the best fighter
- Possesses a nearly unstoppable drive to win
- Can knock an opponent down with a single strike
- Has mastered the powerful Hadoken attack, a surging wave of energy shot from his hands

Orphaned at birth, Ryu was taken in by martial arts master Gouken to a secret training camp, where Ryu began honing his skills as a martial artist.

Ryu became a powerful yet quiet and humble figure, driven only to become a better fighter and to help those in need. For a number of years, Ryu trained with another young man. Ken was the son of a rich American who was friends with Gouken. Ryu and Ken formed a fast bond in training, with Ryu being the persistent, cool-headed student and Ken the fiery, impatient Westerner.

Ryu, wearing a traditional white gi and red gloves, fought his way to the finals of the World Warrior tournament using his distinctive moves: the terrifying Hadoken energy wave, the powerful Shoryuken dragon punch, and the spinning hurricane kick called Tatsumaki Senpukyaku. In the final round, he was nearly defeated by the tournament champion, Sagat. But at the last second, Ryu unconsciously channeled a dark power and hit Sagat in the chest with a vicious Metsu Shoryuken—and won the tournament.

In *Street Fighter II*, Ryu returns home, where he discovers that Gouken has been murdered. Seeking vengeance, Ryu goes in search of Akuma, the man who allegedly killed Gouken. It is through Akuma that Ryu learns he has a dark power with the potential to do great damage—even kill. Ryu continues to struggle with his dark side, sometimes losing control.

Strengths

- Complete confidence in his abilities
- A master Ansatsuken martial artist
- Willingness to fight anyone, anytime
- Dedicated to those he loves
- Expert at combination moves
- Incredible speed of attack

KEN
The Flamboyant American Master with a Pure Heart

Ken Masters is the son of a wealthy American hotel mogul who, deciding that his son needed training and discipline, sent Ken to his old friend Gouken.

Initially, Ken was not thrilled with this arrangement, but he grew to respect his master and dedicated himself to the martial arts. He also became fast friends with Ryu, whose calm and cautious personality provided a good counterpoint to Ken's rash, fearless demeanor.

After years of training, Ken and Ryu were sent out to hone their skills against the best martial artists they could find. Ryu competed in the World Warrior tournament, while Ken returned to America. There, in his trademark red gi, Ken competed in tournament after tournament, winning nearly all of them and becoming an even mightier warrior.

Ken's fighting style is similar to that of his friend and rival Ryu, but he developed greater speed and more complex moves. Ken's power is evident in his flaming Shoryuken punch and multi-hit Tatsumaki Senpukyaku kick. He is known to move dangerously close to his opponents and pummel them with almost unstoppable combination moves.

THE OTHER FIGHTERS

Though Ryu and Ken are the protagonists of the Street Fighter story, the games are full of other combat masters, each of which has gained a following among players. There are more than 60 fighters in the Street Fighter universe, but those from *Street Fighter II* are among the most iconic, both in the series and in video games in general:

AKUMA

NATIONALITY: Japanese

Akuma is a powerful fighter who uses the Ansatsuken style like Ken and Ryu but fully embraces the dark force known as the Satsui No Hadou, which he uses to perform the deadly Raging Demon attack.

BLANKA

NATIONALITY: Brazilian

Blanka is a unique character in that he is not quite human, being green, feral, and having electric powers. He gained these features and his abilities when he was in a plane crash in Brazil, after which he adapted to the wilderness. His style is as animalistic as he is, and he is completely self-taught and wild.

CAMMY

NATIONALITY: British

Cammy represents the might and training of the British secret service as she carries out missions with her trademark double-braided hairstyle. Her fighting is all about being fast and up close to the opponent. She keeps them on their heels while she beats them to a pulp.

CHUN-LI

NATIONALITY: **Chinese**

Chun-Li is one of the most popular characters of the *Street Fighter* series, along with Ryu and Ken. She is blazing fast with her kung fu–style fighting. Her Hyakuretsukyaku lightning kick, which blasts the opponent with kick after kick, is one of the game's most iconic moves.

DHALSIM

NATIONALITY: **Indian**

It might be weird to think that a pacifist and yogi is one of the most popular characters in a video fighting game, but it makes sense when you learn that the long-range fighter Dhalsim enters martial arts contests to earn money for his village. Dhalsim's style is based on the Mysteries of the Yoga and allows him to stretch his limbs and other body parts to tremendous distances to slam his foes with attacks.

GUILE

NATIONALITY: **American**

Guile is a military martial artist who uses kickboxing and pro wrestling moves on his opponents. Guile's trademark hair is a holdover from his military work, and he enters the series as a force for good, trying to avenge M. Bison's killing of his friend.

M. BISON

NATIONALITY: **Unknown**

The dastardly M. Bison is the leader of the evil crime syndicate Shadaloo. His objective is world domination. Bison's style is one that draws on the dangerous forces of Psycho Power. He will hurt anyone in his path—and often does—so many of the characters in the game have personal vendettas against him.

STREET FIGHTER II

SHOWDOWN

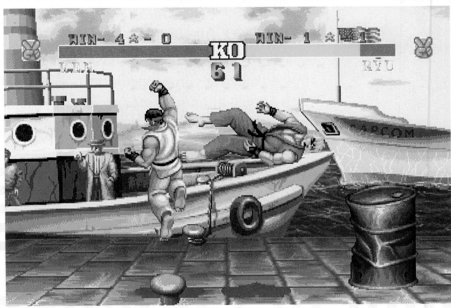

STREET FIGHTER II

Although Ken and Ryu have fought countless times, both in the ring and as sparring partners, their most iconic battle comes in *Street Fighter II,* when Ken finds Ryu in a state of darkness and despair after learning that Akuma has killed their master.

Ryu has just fought Akuma and lost badly. He now knows that, like Akuma, he has Satsui No Hadou, a supernatural power that changes fighters, making them merciless and deadly. The Satsui No Hadou has been known to consume those who possess it. It was this power that enabled Ryu to defeat Sagat in the World Warrior tournament, in which he nearly killed his opponent and left him scarred forever. When Ken finds him, Ryu is in a deep depression.

In an attempt to shake Ryu out of his funk and lead him back to a path of clarity and goodness—and a desire to test himself against such a skilled warrior—Ken challenges his longtime friend to a match.

The battle begins reluctantly for Ryu. But he quickly regains focus when Ken nails him with a fast Hadoken. The two close in on each other and begin fighting in earnest. At first, the two adversaries are almost mirror images of each other.

But the trained eye can see the difference in their blinding attacks: Ryu throws single, powerful blows mixed in with the Shoryuken, while Ken goes for quick combos of many blows. First, Ryu lands one to the head, then Ken strikes Ryu's body multiple times in quick succession. Each fighter backs off for a minute to stare down his friend and rival . . .

Who will win this test of friends? Will the deadly force within Ryu come out in a burst of power, or will Ken earn a victory against his conflicted pal and return him to the true path? Only you can decide, when you play *Street Fighter II*! Or, start a new story and check out Ryu, Chun-Li, M. Bison, and many others in the newest title in the series, *Street Fighter V*!

©CAPCOM

31

Has there ever been a more epic rivalry in all of vide
gaming than that of Hyrule's savior, Link, and the Great King of Evil, Ganondorf
These two have battled with each other across time and dimensions, spannin
centuries and many different games with their mighty conflict. In no figh
however, were the stakes higher and the battle fiercer than *The Legend of Zeld*
Ocarina of Time, considered by many to be one of the greatest games of all tim
(and which got a fancy 3D remake in recent years!).

Images courtesy of Nintendo.

LINK vs. GANONDORF

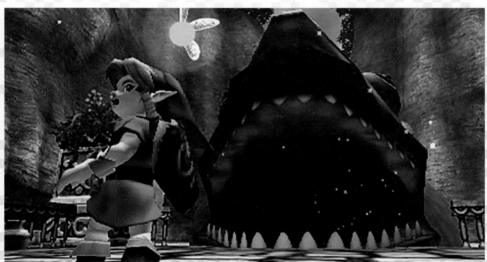

Images courtesy of Nintendo.

Strengths

- Wielder of the Master Sword

- Many other weapons, including Light Arrows and the Megaton Hammer

- Has friends on his side, like the magical Princess Zelda and the fairy Navi

- Has the power of the Triforce of Courage

LINK

The Hylian savior of Hyrule, the Hero of Time

Link is the eternal savior of Hyrule, called to defend his homelands and his universe time and time again. His skills with the sword and the bow (and sometimes the boomerang) are unmatched. His courage is boundless. In fact, Link can wield the actual power of bravery through the Triforce of Courage, whose symbol glows on his hand like a beacon of hope.

In *The Legend of Zelda: Ocarina of Time,* Link zips back and forth through time and space, trying to put right the chaos and destruction wrought by the evil Ganondorf on Link's beloved home, Hyrule. Link's collection of powers and weapons has grown, and his greatest strength is his ability to wield the fabled Master Sword against his enemies. Although Link has battled many creatures—from skeletons and thieves to the sizzling Flare Dancer and powerful Twinrova—his most dangerous quest is to save Princess Zelda, who was captured and imprisoned in crystal. Link must call upon all his powers to save the princess and all of Hyrule from Ganondorf before it's too late . . .

Strengths

- A mighty warrior with many spells at his disposal

- Nearly invulnerable to damage, except by very powerful weapons

- Holder of the terrifying and destructive Triforce of Power

- Has tremendous strength

- Transforms into his bestial form, the dread Ganon

GANONDORF
The Great King of Evil, the Dark Lord

You can tell just from that list above that Ganondorf is one mean, dangerous dude. Ganondorf has been battling Link throughout the ages. He sure can hold a grudge!

Perhaps in no era of the Legend of Zelda series was Ganondorf ever so powerful or so close to becoming the eternal king of Hyrule than in *The Legend of Zelda: Ocarina of Time*. Ganondorf is so bad and so powerful in this game that he actually does manage to touch the Triforce and use it to turn all of Hyrule into a place of death, darkness, and chaos. However, as his heart is not balanced, the Triforce splits into three pieces as told by prophecies, so though Ganondorf is nearly immortal and impossible to kill, he needs to get the Triforce back together to become truly all powerful. That's when he snatches up Princess Zelda, holder of the Triforce of Wisdom, and not too long after, Link shows up . . .

SHOWDOWN

As Link enters the yawning, cavernous room at the top of Ganondorf's tower, the evil king acts as if he doesn't see him. Instead, Ganondorf focuses on playing his theme song on a massive organ, like a true boss. It's only when he's finished playing that Ganondorf calmly turns around, laughing that Link has brought him the final piece of the Triforce, which begins to glow on Link's hand.

Suddenly, Ganondorf spews waves of darkness at Link that even the fairy Navi can't handle. He flies into the air and slams back down, destroying a large part of the floor. Link has to act quickly, as Ganondorf starts slinging balls of crackling lightning at him.

With great balls of lightning firing all around him, Link first tries to dodge the danger. But as pieces of the floor start dropping away, Link realizes that he must do something to disrupt Ganondorf's attacks, or he'll be toast. Thinking fast, Link slams his Master Sword at one of the lightning balls, batting it back at Ganondorf. A ferocious game of lightning tennis ensues, with one fighter knocking the lightning at the other until, finally, Ganondorf's concentration slips for an instant and he is hit by his own spell.

Images courtesy of Nintendo.

Taking advantage of the momentary weakness, Link blasts a Light Arrow into Ganondorf. He leaps across the chasm, bringing his trusty blade down in a tremendous attack on the reeling Ganondorf. The Dark Lord falls, grasping his throat as his life force spills out, incredulous that he has been beaten by a mere teenager. But just as he seems about to perish, and Link starts to feel the swell of triumph rise within him, something happens . . .

Gandondorf raises his arms to the heavens, and his whole body crackles with lightning. The building is coming down! Link and Zelda rush to escape. Lava spews all around, and skeleton-like creatures called Stalfos attack them as they run. Link and Princess Zelda barely make it out, when stones from the tower collapse in a mighty rush. Once again, it seems to be over.

But they are mistaken.

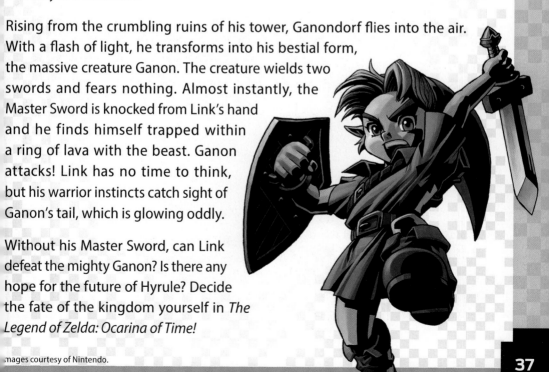

Rising from the crumbling ruins of his tower, Ganondorf flies into the air. With a flash of light, he transforms into his bestial form, the massive creature Ganon. The creature wields two swords and fears nothing. Almost instantly, the Master Sword is knocked from Link's hand and he finds himself trapped within a ring of lava with the beast. Ganon attacks! Link has no time to think, but his warrior instincts catch sight of Ganon's tail, which is glowing oddly.

Without his Master Sword, can Link defeat the mighty Ganon? Is there any hope for the future of Hyrule? Decide the fate of the kingdom yourself in *The Legend of Zelda: Ocarina of Time!*

THE MASTER CHIEF

The long war against the Covenant produced many heroes, but only one legend. That legend began as a young boy named John, who would be enhanced, trained, and encased in advanced Mjolnir powered armor, ultimately becoming the Master Chief. For three decades, the Master Chief has battled against the Covenant, eventually making the critical discovery of Halo and tipping the scales in humanity's favor. In addition, his unlikely alliance with the Elite commander known as the Arbiter would ensure peace between the Elites and humanity after the war.

THE SPARTANS

The Spartans are super-soldiers trained from youth to be a shield wielded in the defense of humanity. Always outnumbered but never outmatched, Spartans wear advanced Mjolnir powered armor, which improves their already incredible reflexes, strength, and speed, making each one as powerful as a tank.

THE COVENANT

The Covenant is an alliance of alien species founded in the hopes of securing knowledge of their gods, the long-lost Forerunners, and the divine methods by which they had transcended physical existence. Central to the Covenant's ultimate goal was the search for Halo, an array of ancient ringworlds that were believed to be the means by which the Forerunners had transformed themselves into divine beings. The search for the secrets of the Forerunners and the Halo rings was known as the Great Journey. For hundreds of years the Covenant scoured the galaxy for Halo, finding many lost Forerunner installations and relics along the way.

The discovery of humanity and revelations that the Forerunners had intended to leave stewardship of the galaxy in our hands threatened the very foundation of the Covenant and its promise of salvation. Quickly hiding this information, the Covenant leadership decided that they had no choice but to destroy humanity and prevent anyone from discovering the truth. And so, the mighty armies and fleets of the Covenant went to war based on a lie.

THE ELITES

Obsessed with honor and warfare, the Elites (or "Sangheili," as they called themselves) were tasked by the Covenant leadership with winning the war on humanity. Though they could be ruthless and without mercy, the Elites' strong code of honor forced them to recognize humanity as a worthy foe and to question the wisdom of their misguided orders. As doubt spread in the ranks, the Covenant began to fracture as humanity was pushed to the edge of defeat.

SHOWDOWN

The alien alliance known as the Covenant advances on Earth, destroying every colony and human fleet in its way. On a forlorn planet, the United Nations Space Command clashes with Covenant forces, and the Master Chief is at the front lines. Plasma and tracer fire arcs across the sky, and the fate of the world lies in the balance. The Master Chief is on foot, the burning wreckage of his Warthog truck behind him.

Arrayed against Earth's hero is a full legion of Covenant warriors guarding a landing zone. Dropships land as Elites bark orders to cowering Grunts, and savage Brutes ignore their orders and spread out to plunder the battlefield. The full might of the Covenant is on display as they prepare to advance on the last human forces grimly holding the line. Failure is not an option, but victory seems impossible. With other forces in retreat, only the Master Chief remains to blunt the aliens' attack.

As rain begins to fall and extinguishes the Warthog's guttering flames, the Master Chief advances, using the weather and terrain to close in on the enemy camp unseen and unheard. In his mind he creates a hundred battle plans, a thousand possible tactical maneuvers. He sees the Covenant commander standing atop a watchtower, clad in gold armor and purple cloak, directing the alien war machine efficiently and without a shred of pity.

Defeating the commander will not disrupt the Covenant invasion plans for long, but it will buy valuable hours that the human forces can use to regroup and form a stronger defense. The Master Chief considers his options as lighting cracks open the sky, briefly revealing the massive bulk of Covenant warships descending below the clouds to disgorge fresh legions into the fight. The Master Chief calculates the odds and makes a decision as he unslings his assault rifle and checks his ammunition supply. He has only one chance at success.

The Covenant leader surveys the surrounding terrain, emotionless and alert.

Will the Master Chief triumph this day, engulfing the alien forces in confusion and dismay? Or will the Covenant foil the Master Chief's plans and bring this world under its control? Alien warlord versus Spartan super-soldier in an epic clash of will and firepower: You decide the outcome.

The Pokémon series is about Pokémon Trainers doing two things: catching them all (the adorable Pokémon, that is!), and becoming the battle champion of the region by pitting their wits and Pokémon against the Elite Four and then the dreaded regional League Champion.

It is no easy task: It takes a tremendous amount of passion and dedication, not to mention some seriously tough Pokémon, to reach the regional levels of the Pokémon League. Trainers not only have to catch and train different types of Pokémon, they also have to find, battle, and beat the Gym Leaders—powerful Pokémon Trainers who are champions at the local city level.

Only when a Trainer has beaten all the Gym Leaders will he or she face the Elite Four, the greatest Trainers in the region. And once those four are done? Well, that's when the real fight begins, as the League Champion steps forward to give the Trainer the fight of his or her life.

Fighting the Elite Four and the League Champion is one of the great challenges in video gaming. Since the first Pokémon games came out, millions have battled their way through multiple regions of the Pokémon world to accomplish their personal goals and add their names to the Pokémon Hall of Fame.

Although there is a Pokémon League for each region, our showdown takes place against the Elite Four of Sinnoh and their League Champion, Cynthia, as seen in the popular *Pokémon Platinum* edition.

THE POKÉMON TRAINER VS. THE ELITE FOUR AND LEAGUE CHAMPION

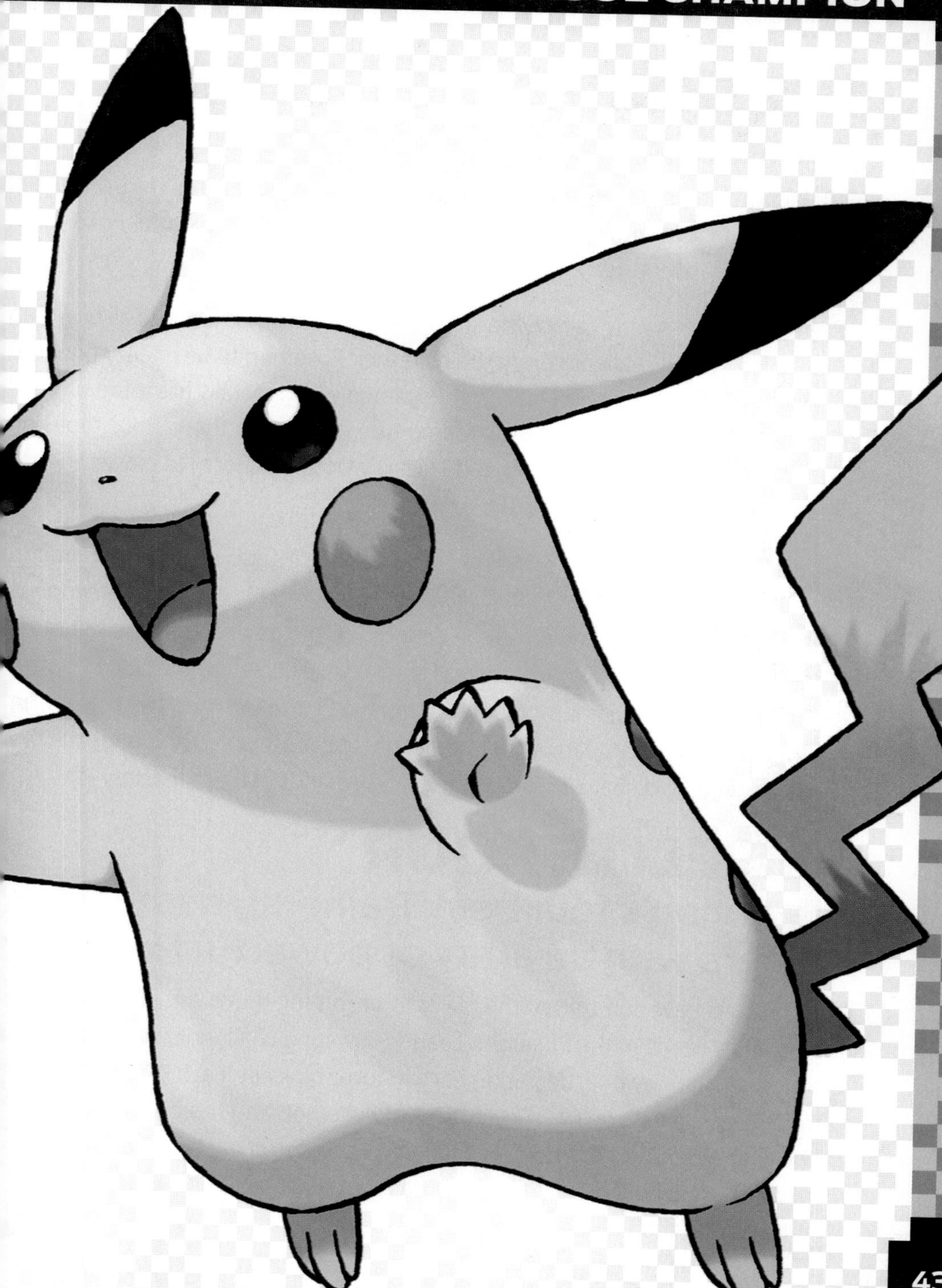

THE POKÉMON TRAINER
The kid who wants to be Champion

All Pokémon Trainers start their journeys at a young age, setting out from their hometowns on foot with nothing but a little money, their trusty starter Pokémon, and a sense of adventure.

By the time they're ready to face the Elite Four, the Trainer has traveled all over the region, taking on all challengers and training their Pokémon to be mighty fighting machines. A Trainer who treats his or her Pokémon well generally has more success than one who doesn't. They must become true experts on the various types of Pokémon—including their strengths and weaknesses—and learn to master the art of battle strategy.

It is a challenging process not for the faint of heart—but it's also incredibly rewarding. As the Trainer steps off Victory Road in *Pokémon Platinum* and enters the tremendous building that is home to the Pokémon League, he or she must choose the most trusted and powerful Pokémon if there is any hope of defeating the Elite Four and League Champion. Each attempt at becoming the Champion must be undertaken with the same Pokémon team, so the Trainer has to choose wisely and hope they've trained enough, or defeat will come swiftly at the hands of these masters.

THE ELITE FOUR
The region's four best Trainers; master Trainers with an array of powerful Pokémor

These masters have committed their lives to becoming dominant Pokémon fighters. They reside in the Pokémon League, awaiting challengers who must take them on, one by one, defeating each in turn. Typically, each Elite Four member specializes in one particular type of Pokémon and has built a team around that type. This forces any Trainer who wishes to challenge the Elite Four to build a team of Pokémon that is highly adaptable and capable of taking on any type of Pokémon in the world.

The Elite Four of Sinnoh, found in *Pokémon Diamond, Pearl,* and *Platinum,* have a daunting roster of master Trainers, including:

Aaron: The Bug-type Trainer

Aaron is a young kid with laser-green hair and a prominent cowlick in the middle of his head. He hangs out in a room fit for his beloved Bug-type Pokémon, with grass, rocks, and logs for them to play in. He thinks Bug-types are both beautiful and dangerous.

Aaron's team:
Yanmega • Scizor • Vespiquen • Heracross • Drapion

Bertha: Master of the Ground-type Pokémon

Bertha is the oldest member of the Sinnoh Elite Four. Her gray hair is evidence of the many years she has trained to become the best Ground-type Trainer in Sinnoh. She waits for challengers in a desert-like room, wearing her big white coat.

Bertha's team:

Whiscash • Gilscor • Hippowdon • Golem • Rhyperior

Flint: Fire Pokémon Trainer with an Attitude

Flint likes a laugh, and his fiery personality is matched by his love for the dangerous Fire-type Pokémon that he uses in battle. His room is fitted with numerous lava pits, which create a warm and comfortable atmosphere for Flint and his team.

Flint's team:

Houndoom • Flareon • Rapidash • Infernape • Magmortar

Lucian: The Mental Master of Psychic Pokémon

Lucian likes to sit in his room and read while waiting for Trainers to come challenge him. Lucian's desire to enhance his mind is no surprise, as all his Pokémon are of the Psychic-type.

Lucian's team:

Mr. Mime • Espeon • Bronzong • Alakazam • Gallade

SHOWDOWN

The Champion and Final Showdown

While defeating the Elite Four might seem tough, it's nothing compared to the task that awaits the Trainer if he or she manages to win. Waiting at the top of the Pokémon League is the best of the best: the Pokémon League Champion. The Champion will put the Trainer to the test like never before, throwing the mightiest and best-trained Pokémon into battle over and over, never giving an easy inch of ground. It is the true test of a Trainer's mettle—and a battle he or she will never forget.

Cynthia: Champion of the Sinnoh Region

The Champion of Sinnoh is Cynthia, which can come as a bit of a surprise to the Pokémon Trainer, as Cynthia is actually a friend who had been helping the Trainer along the path to glory.

Cynthia's team:
Spiritomb • Roserade • Togekiss • Lucario • Milotic • Garchomp

The Showdown

The Pokémon Trainer enters a massive hall full of lights and impressive geometric architecture. Classical piano music fills the space. The Trainer looks up and is surprised to see Cynthia standing at the top of the hall. Cynthia greets the Trainer as a friend, but in this meeting of friends there is much tension, as only one can emerge victorious. Cynthia shakes out her flowing blond hair, and her long black coat billows about her as she challenges the Trainer to one final showdown. Now it is up to you to take up the challenge. Accept the challenge and find out what your Pokémon are truly made of.

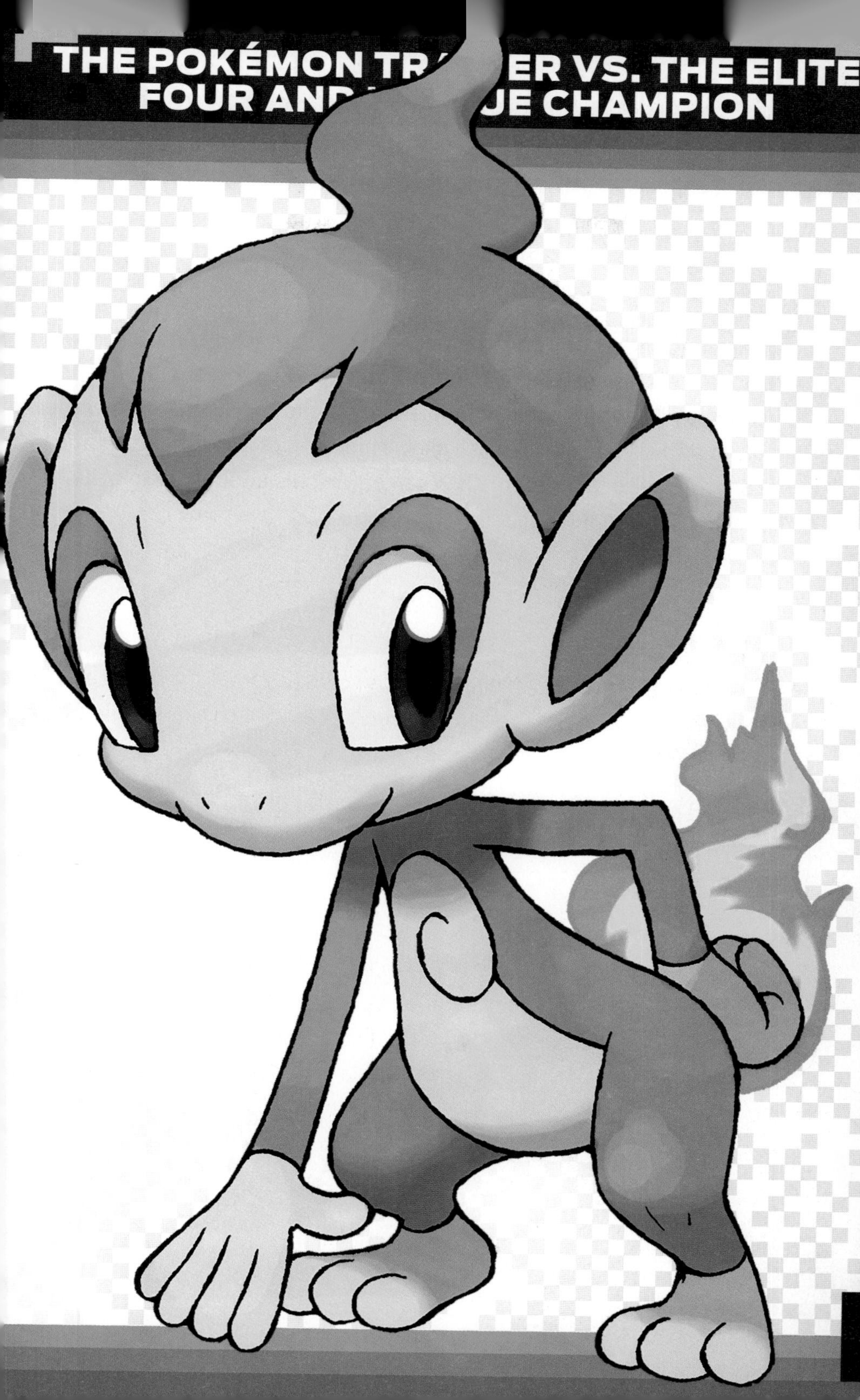

KIRBY vs. KING DEDEDE

It's Kirby! The small pink hero of dozens of video games, dating back to Nintendo's first handheld gaming system, the Game Boy.

Kirby is among the most iconic characters in gaming, partly for his portly pink body, but also for his incredible abilities. Kirby's body is soft and flexible, which allows him to flatten himself or inflate like a balloon. His main power is his tremendous ability to inhale, which allows him to suck up his enemies and just about anything else in his path. Kirby can also inhale enough air to balloon up and float right over danger!

Images courtesy of Nintendo.

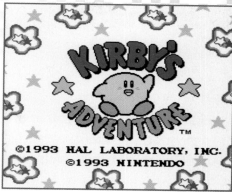

Kirby's abilities have served him well in battles with his archrival, the hammer-wielding King Dedede. Kirby and the king have squared off in more than a dozen games, and their showdowns have become the stuff of video-game legends.

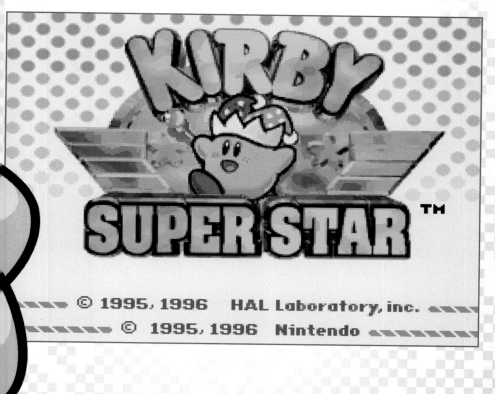

Strengths

- Can inhale just about anything
- Takes on the powers of enemies he inhales
- Floats like a balloon when he inhales air
- Exhales air to fight back enemies
- Can sometimes wield weapons, such as hammers and swords

KIRBY
Star Warrior, Savior of Dream Land

A force for good and justice, Kirby lives in a domed house in Dream Land, a country on the planet Popstar. Kirby often finds his homeland in danger, usually due to the actions of his nemesis, King Dedede, the self-proclaimed king of Dream Land.

Kirby's biggest strength lies in his ability to consume just about anything—including his enemies. Sometimes Kirby can copy or temporarily embody the abilities of the person or thing inhaled, making him even more dangerous to bad guys.

Kirby has a great skill set, and his abilities are among the most memorable in gaming. But they are also talents Kirby has needed time and time again in confrontations with the greedy King Dedede.

Strengths

- Controls a large number of fortresses across games

- Has many minions in various forms, but particularly the Waddle Dees

- Wields a mighty giant hammer that has different capabilities

- Just like Kirby, can inhale to float and suck in enemies, although he doesn't gain their powers

- More, depending on the game

KING DEDEDE
The King of Dream Land (or so he says!)

King Dedede is the penguin-like guy who carries a big hammer and thinks he is the biggest, best thing in Dream Land. King Dedede is always making trouble, whether it's stealing all the food in Dream Land to keep for himself or being brainwashed by more powerful villains.

In general, King Dedede tries to use his minions and underbosses to get rid of Kirby, so he can commit some greedy, self-centered deed. When his underlings fail, King Dedede often combats Kirby himself.

53

KIRBY vs. KING DEDEDE

SHOWDOWN

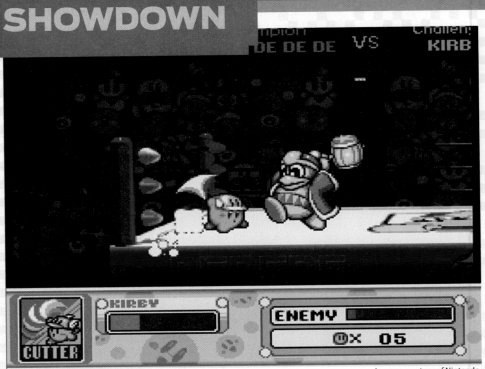

Images courtesy of Nintendo.

The ultimate showdown between Kirby and King Dedede started off in *Kirby's Dream Land* and was re-created in later games. Perhaps the best fight takes place in the segment known as "Revenge of the King," in *Kirby Super Star Ultra*.

Here, Kirby battles through wave after wave of enemies, including a series of tough mini-bosses directed by King Dedede to keep Kirby away from his castle.

Kirby, however, is having none of it and fights all the way to King Dedede. The ever-resourceful King Dedede immediately reveals that he has upgraded his trusted hammer and undergone a few modifications himself. He now has some serious face guard as well as a new and improved megahammer—and he's out to pummel our little pink hero with both!

KIRBY vs. KING DEDEDE

As Kirby enters the palace, he finds himself in the middle of a giant fighting ring complete with cage match. The ring is surrounded by Waddle Dees, cheering on their king. Anticipating what is to come, Kirby picks up a hammer of his own. Frantic music kicks in, and the now mechanized and improved King Dedede steps onto the stage of battle with a bigger, better hammer than ever. King Dedede attempts a wild spinning attack move that nearly knocks Kirby into the bleachers. But Kirby finds that he can float just above the king and land a few blows before the attack begins anew.

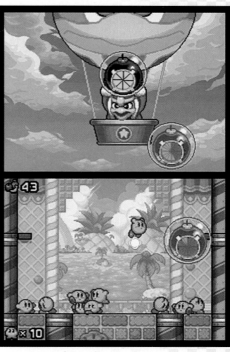

Images courtesy of Nintendo.

The two lifelong antagonists continue the battle. But the question is: With everything on the line for Dream Land, who will win?!

Sounds

by Margie Burton, Cathy French, and Tammy Jones

Shhh-shhh! Listen. What can
you hear?

You may hear people talking,
a car driving by,
or an airplane way up in the sky.
These are all sounds.

I can hear people talking.

I can hear cars.

I can hear airplanes.

Sounds are all around us.

Some sounds are loud.
Trains make loud sounds
as they go down the tracks.

Loud sounds are
easy to hear.

Some sounds are soft. Cats
make soft sounds as they purr.

Soft sounds are hard to hear.

Sounds can be high or low.

Look at the bells.

The big bell makes a low sound.

The small bell makes a high sound.

When you sing, you can make a
low sound or a high sound.

Sound is made when things move back and forth very fast.

Sounds move through the air.

When a bird sings, you
can hear it because the sound
goes through the air.

Sounds move through the water, too.

When the dolphins talk, they
can hear each other because
the sound goes through the water.

We cannot see sounds but we
can hear them.
We use our ears to hear the sounds.

Some sounds help us tell other people what we are thinking.

We can feel the sound when we sing or talk.

Some sounds let us know what is going on.

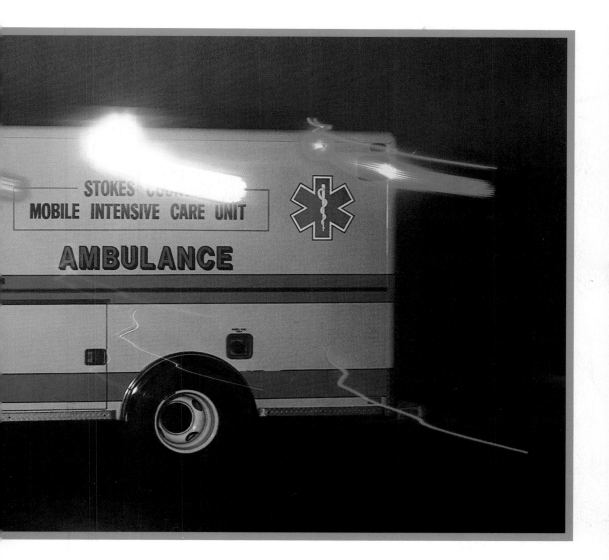

Sounds can help us every day.